Keeping the U.
Relationship M

COUNCIL *on*
FOREIGN
RELATIONS

Center for Preventive Action

Council Special Report No. 81
February 2018

Joshua Kurlantzick

Keeping the U.S.-Indonesia Relationship Moving Forward

Contents

Foreword

Indonesia would seem to be a natural partner for the United States. It is the most populous country in Southeast Asia, a vibrant democracy, a leader of the Association of Southeast Asian Nations (ASEAN), and a member of the Group of Twenty. But as Senior Fellow for Southeast Asia Joshua Kurlantzick asserts in this new Council Special Report, the relationship between the United States and Indonesia "has long underperformed its potential."

Kurlantzick argues that Indonesia could be more of a security partner for the United States and proposes to increase the scope of cooperation in three areas in which the countries have shared interests. First, the United States and Indonesia should work together to check China's growing assertiveness in the South China Sea. Second, the two countries should jointly combat the expansion into Southeast Asia of militants linked to the self-proclaimed Islamic State. And finally, the two countries should cooperate to counter piracy and other transnational crime in Southeast Asia.

The South China Sea, in particular, makes for a good focus for the bilateral relationship in coming years. Indonesia is increasingly worried by China's extensive claims, which also include waters claimed by Indonesia. Indonesia has had three major maritime skirmishes with Chinese vessels in the South China Sea, and it has begun seizing Chinese vessels that it believes are encroaching on Indonesian waters. Indonesia's growing willingness to take a stand in the South China Sea dovetails with the Donald J. Trump administration's regularization of freedom of navigation operations and its articulation of a "free and open Indo-Pacific" aimed at countering China's increasing clout in the region. The United States is also in the market for new partners in this effort, as the Philippines under President Rodrigo Duterte has tilted toward China and chosen not to press its claims in the South China Sea. Indonesia, as a leading voice in ASEAN, is well placed to prod the group to take a more unified position on the South China Sea and adopt a legally bind-ing code of conduct.

While there is scope for cooperation in the security realm, Kur-lantzick is less optimistic about the prospect of upgrading economic ties or working together to promote democracy and human rights. As Kurlantzick notes, both Presidents Trump and Joko Widodo (or Jokowi) are inclined toward economic nationalism and place little emphasis on democracy promotion. The United States and Indone-sia are thus "unlikely to develop the kind of comprehensive bilateral relationship often envisioned" and instead should "attempt to stall any further deterioration of the bilateral economic relationship" and retain any "modest momentum."

Overall, Kurlantzick recommends taking a more transactional approach to the U.S.-Indonesia relationship, which could well be wel-comed by the Trump administration. The three discrete security goals Kurlantzick discusses are in both countries' interests to pursue. More broadly, Kurlantzick demonstrates a realistic appreciation of how both the Trump and Jokowi administrations view the world and offers modest but potentially achievable policy prescriptions for moving the relationship forward in light of that larger context.

Richard N. Haass
President
Council on Foreign Relations
February 2018

Acknowledgments

I would like to express thanks to the people who made this report possible. I thank CFR President Richard N. Haass, Senior Vice President and Director of Studies James M. Lindsay, and General John W. Vessey Senior Fellow for Conflict Prevention and Director of the Center for Preventive Action (CPA) Paul B. Stares for their support of this project, their feedback, and their analysis of the research and writing. I also want to thank all the members of the study group on the future of U.S.-Indonesia relations, who contributed valuable insights and extensive notes on initial drafts. I particularly want to thank Ambassador Cameron Hume, chair of the study group. I also want to thank Patricia Dorff, Julie Hersh, and Sumit Poudyal in CFR Publications for their editorial support, CFR Digital Design, and Communications. I also would like to thank Research Associate James West and former CPA Assistant Director Helia Ighani for all their work in helping produce this report. This publication was made possible by a generous grant from Carnegie Corporation of New York. The statements made and views expressed are solely my own.

Joshua Kurlantzick

Council Special Report

Introduction

The relationship between the United States and Indonesia has long underperformed its potential. Indonesia could be a critical security partner and a larger location for U.S. investment and trade in the next few years. The policies of Susilo Bambang Yudhoyono's administration in the 2000s and early 2010s seemed about to usher in greater bilateral cooperation, including upgraded economic links, but both Washington and Jakarta overestimated how quickly the relationship would expand. Despite growing strategic relations between the United States and Indonesia, the U.S. armed forces have less comprehensive ties with the Indonesian military than they do with many other militaries in Southeast Asia, and the economic relationship has made only limited progress, despite growing U.S. investment.

The two sides now face significant obstacles to a closer relationship that would encompass not only strategic ties but also deeper economic ties and cooperation in promoting rights and democracy. With the Donald J. Trump administration concerned about trade imbalances with major exporters, the White House might focus on what it perceives to be unfair trade relationships with Indonesia, which would anger Indonesians.[1] The Trump administration has also downplayed democracy and human rights as core components of U.S. foreign policy.[2] Yudhoyono's successor, President Joko Widodo, or Jokowi, has himself advocated less for regional democracy promotion efforts than his predecessor did. Given these obstacles, the United States and Indonesia are unlikely to develop the kind of comprehensive bilateral relationship often envisioned—but never fully achieved—in the 2000s and early 2010s.

Instead of seeking unlikely goals, the two nations should embrace a more transactional approach. The relationship should focus on three clear, shared security challenges: China's growing assertiveness in the South China Sea, which contests U.S. primacy and potentially hampers

Indonesian access to South China Sea waters; the expansion of militants linked to the self-proclaimed Islamic State into Southeast Asia, which threatens Indonesia and the halt of which is a White House priority; and piracy in Southeast Asia, which disrupts Indonesia's stability and funds militant groups. Such a practical and security-based approach should appeal to both nations' presidents.

Meanwhile, the United States and Indonesia should strive for modest but achievable improvements in economic relations in the next few years, before the next U.S. and Indonesian presidential elections, in 2020 and 2019, respectively. Although achieving modest improvements may seem like limited progress, it is far preferable to another potential outcome of the economic relationship—rising bilateral trade barriers and aggressive economic nationalism on both sides.

The United States and a Democratic Indonesia: History, Hopes, and Hurdles

During the Suharto era, from 1967 to 1998, Indonesia, the most populous state in Southeast Asia, led the Association of Southeast Asian Nations (ASEAN). Jakarta regularly set policy direction for the organization and for Southeast Asia in general. The United States and Indonesia built up close military-to-military relations and strong ties between top economic policymakers. Suharto's government welcomed foreign investment—although its corruption and political repression ultimately made it an unstable partner.

After more than thirty years of authoritarian rule under Suharto, Indonesia's political system and economy unraveled in the 1990s, badly damaging its domestic stability. This unraveling also undercut its primacy in the region, because Indonesia's leaders became almost totally focused on its domestic political and economic crises. During the latter years of the Suharto regime, the United States also cut off nearly all military links to the Indonesian armed forces after revelations of the Indonesian military's abuses in the then-province of East Timor and other parts of the archipelago. The Asian financial crisis seriously damaged Indonesia's economy, which shrank by 13 percent in 1998.[3] In the chaos, Indonesia became a pariah for many foreign investors. Suharto's regime collapsed amid massive street protests over his administration's alleged corruption and the effects of the financial crisis on ordinary Indonesians. In May 1998, Suharto handed power to his vice president, B. J. Habibie.

Habibie proved more of a reformist than many opponents had expected: he oversaw the beginnings of a transition to democracy and what would become one of the most far-reaching experiments in political decentralization in Asia.

Indonesia's democratic transition was one of the most impressive in the world, at both national and local levels. The country held multiple free elections on all levels, including for many local legislatures and governorships that had previously been appointed.[4] The military did not retake control of the government, unlike in neighboring Thailand, even though Indonesia suffered from instability. It faced separatist movements in the late 1990s and 2000s, as well as a spate of terrorist attacks led by the al-Qaeda-linked group Jemaah Islamiyah.

The process of democratization allowed the United States to rebuild some security ties with Indonesia, but they never reached the levels they had in the Suharto era. Following the 9/11 attacks, as combating terrorist networks became a U.S. policy priority, the United States resumed limited military aid to Indonesia, including training and nonlethal equipment sales.[5] Washington restored full defense ties in 2005, and the Barack Obama administration later expanded training of Indonesian military forces.[6] However, Indonesia and the United States still had only limited intelligence sharing on militant groups and modest military cooperation on nontraditional security challenges, including piracy.

Habibie's successors as president, the cleric Abdurrahman Wahid and the former opposition leader Megawati Sukarnoputri, proved ineffective politicians. When the former general Yudhoyono was elected president in 2004, he vowed to crack down on terrorism, improve the country's investment climate, fight corruption, and help regain the country's status as a regional and international power—a shift the United States supported.

In office, Yudhoyono tried to rebuild Indonesia's credibility as the natural leader of Southeast Asia. He took the lead, with varying amounts of success, on regional challenges from Myanmar's political reforms to combating climate change. He focused on holding up Indonesia as a political success story, and (at first) on demonstrating that Indonesia welcomed investment. Indonesia joined the Group of Twenty. With U.S. support, Yudhoyono oversaw the 2008 launch of the Bali Democracy Forum, an annual event that brings leaders together to share ideas about how to make free political systems work.[7]

Domestically, a new elite counterterrorism force, supported by the United States and Australia, helped dismantle Jemaah Islamiyah. This success could be the reason that some Indonesian politicians, including Yudhoyono, became complacent about the ongoing threat of radical movements in the archipelago, which persisted even as Jemaah Islamiyah was badly damaged.

Yudhoyono also wooed foreign investors, and his administration pushed Indonesia toward manufactured exports and other value-added goods and services. As Yudhoyono touted Indonesia's economic stability in the 2000s and early 2010s, the country's economy recovered somewhat from the Asian financial crisis and began regularly posting growth rates of over 5 percent.

Yudhoyono enunciated a foreign policy doctrine in which Indonesia would have "a million friends and zero enemies." This was an update to Jakarta's traditional nonalignment principle. Indonesia would now work with all major powers and play a larger role in shaping the regional order.[8] But it still kept Indonesia essentially neutral, and often passive, on issues related to the South China Sea, with Jakarta hoping to play a mediator role among the United States, China, and Southeast Asia.

During Yudhoyono's two terms (he was reelected in 2009), the U.S. government and U.S. investors attempted to rebuild a close relationship with Indonesia. In 2010, the two nations signed a comprehensive partnership designed to provide a framework for closer security and economic links, and people-to-people ties.[9] The Obama administration followed the partnership with the U.S.-Indonesia Strategic Partnership in 2015 (completed during Jokowi's presidency).[10] U.S. officials, and some members of Yudhoyono's administration, hoped to use these partnerships to push Indonesia to assume an even larger regional role on major issues, including resurgent Islamist militant groups and rising instability in the South China Sea. Yet because of Indonesia's neutrality, the new partnership did not dramatically upgrade the U.S.-Indonesia relationship.

A closer economic bilateral relationship remained stalled as well. Yudhoyono's second term was clouded by corruption scandals.[11] Even as he fostered a more stable macroeconomic climate, the high level of graft undermined entrepreneurial activity.[12] U.S. investment increased in Indonesia during Yudhoyono's terms but still lagged behind U.S. investment in other regional economies, such as Malaysia and Thailand.[13]

Sensing heightened public anger that growth had not addressed Indonesia's inequality, Yudhoyono began to adopt more nationalist policies in his second term. He oversaw new nontariff barriers and the passage of laws restricting foreign investment in oil services, retail sectors, some power plants, and other industries.[14] By the time Yudhoyono left office in 2014, his attempts to prod Indonesia to a bigger regional and global leadership role had produced only mixed results, despite the country's democratic consolidation and decent economic growth.

Jokowi and Today's Common U.S.-Indonesia Interests

Hurdles to Indonesia's economic resurgence—and to closer ties between the United States and Indonesia on economic and democracy-related issues—became more evident during and after the Indonesian presidential election of 2014. Both candidates, Jokowi and former Lieutenant General Prabowo Subianto, vowed on the campaign trail to strengthen Indonesia's state-owned enterprises, bolster state spending, and enact new regulations on foreign investment.[15] Although Jokowi spoke of his commitment to Indonesian democracy, he did not emphasize democracy promotion.

After Jokowi won the election, he outlined nine priorities for his administration. Among them was a promise to cut red tape to make it easier for businesses to operate in Indonesia. But he also planned to continue limits on foreign ownership in some economic sectors as well as to create new regulations on foreign investors in extractive industries. Jokowi initially made it clear that he would approach foreign relations differently than Yudhoyono, and not only on democracy issues. Jokowi came into office "less oriented toward multilateralism in general" and less interested in being seen as a global leader, although he has not totally abandoned speaking about Indonesia's democratic successes.[16]

Jokowi's reticence on rights issues now coincides with the approach of the Trump administration, which has focused on an interests-based and sovereignty-oriented foreign policy. In a September 2017 speech to the UN General Assembly, Trump highlighted the importance of sovereignty in international relations, telling attendees, "We do not expect diverse countries to share the same cultures, traditions, or even systems of government."[17] Trump enunciated similar themes at a speech to the Asia-Pacific Economic Cooperation (APEC) summit in Vietnam in November 2017.[18]

Instead of broad attempts to gain global leadership and promote a values-based foreign policy, the Jokowi administration initially focused on protecting narrow national interests, such as maintaining Indonesia's exclusive economic zone in the South China Sea waters surrounding its Natuna archipelago.[19] Early in his first term, Jokowi did not seem to believe that either resurgent Islamist radicalism or Beijing's approach to the South China Sea was a major threat to Indonesia's security. He did suggest that Indonesia would increase its military budget to 1.5 percent of its gross domestic product within five years.[20] However, Jokowi's initial vision for the budget seemed confused—it focused on upgrading Indonesia's port infrastructure more than its weapons systems.[21]

The Indonesian military's navy and coast guard are badly outdated; this became especially apparent in 2016 and 2017 as Indonesian leaders became increasingly concerned about how Beijing's South China Sea approach will broadly affect Indonesia. The country's armed forces still lag behind regional peers such as the Vietnamese military in equipment and integration of forces, which makes it even more difficult for Jakarta to defend its exclusive economic zones and, potentially, freedom of navigation in regional waters.[22]

However, in the past two years, the Jokowi administration has begun to take three major security threats more seriously: potential conflict in the South China Sea, the growth of militant groups linked to the Islamic State, and maritime piracy. On these three issues, Washington and Jakarta now share significant common interests, creating the potential for joint action to address them.

SOUTH CHINA SEA

For one, China's increasing assertiveness in the South China Sea has become far more apparent to Indonesian opinion leaders. This assertiveness includes a pace of land reclamation and militarization that has exceeded projections of even the most pessimistic Southeast Asian observers five years earlier. In 2016, Beijing for the first time asserted that some waters claimed by Indonesia came within China's vast "nine-dash line" definition of Chinese waters in the South China Sea.[23]

In the past year, Indonesia has had three major maritime skirmishes with Chinese vessels in the South China Sea. The Jokowi government has also begun seizing Chinese vessels that it believes are encroaching on Indonesian waters.[24] With this encroachment, Beijing is threatening waters near the Indonesian Natuna Islands. But Indonesian officials are also more generally worried that China will soon be able to completely control boat traffic in the South China Sea. Indonesian security specialists and military officers have watched in 2016 and 2017 as some Southeast Asian nations—most notably, the Philippines under President Rodrigo Duterte—appear to have largely accepted that China will eventually dominate the South China Sea.

These factors have caused many Indonesian opinion leaders to conclude that Indonesia needs a broader, tougher South China Sea strategy. This strategy would include more effective deterrence beyond simply protecting waters near the Natunas—it would also recognize Indonesia's broad interest in protecting freedom of navigation, fishing rights, and other common freedoms in the South China Sea.

Reflecting shifting views in Jakarta about how to handle the South China Sea, in 2016 and 2017 the Jokowi administration took a more expansive approach to its South China Sea policy. Since early 2016, the Jokowi administration has held several military exercises in the South China Sea, in a warning that it will be taking a more assertive posture. Indonesia has also been firing warning shots at Chinese vessels it believes are encroaching on Indonesian waters.

In July 2017, the Jokowi administration decreed that the Indonesian government would start referring to an area of the waters as the North Natuna Sea rather than the South China Sea, a typical regional rhetorical strategy for pushing back against Chinese influence.[25] Indonesian officials have also spoken out publicly about the need for all parties to accept freedom of navigation in the South China Sea and have prepared to regularly deploy warships there.

The Trump administration, meanwhile, has made an assertive South China Sea approach central to its Asia strategy. The administration has reportedly created a schedule of regular freedom of navigation operations (FONOPs) in the South China Sea; the previous administration used these operations only irregularly.[26] The White House also appears willing to demonstrate a deterrent posture in the South China Sea alongside major allies; in 2017, the Trump administration conducted an exercise in the South China Sea with Japan's biggest warship, which was the first time the United States and Japan had conducted an exercise of this size there.[27] The White House has also upped rhetorical warnings to Beijing not to continue its pace of militarization and land reclamation. These warnings have come from Secretary of Defense Jim Mattis, at the annual Shangri-La Dialogue in Singapore, and from the president himself, who decried what he called a "threat to sovereignty" in the South China Sea.[28]

ISLAMIST MILITANCY

The second major security threat that the Jokowi administration appears increasingly worried by is Islamist militancy. The United States is also focusing on Southeast Asia as a growing front for Islamic State–linked militants. Militant groups—those involved in popular politics as well as those carrying out violent attacks—have reemerged as potent forces within Indonesia, despite the Yudhoyono administration's successes in dismantling Jemaah Islamiyah.

In the past two years, militants have used social media to organize large rallies that influenced elections within Indonesia. Throughout late 2016 and early 2017, militant Islamist groups rallied hundreds of thousands in Jakarta to oppose the election of Basuki Tjahaja Purnama, or Ahok, an ethnically Chinese Christian Indonesian, as governor of Jakarta. The rallies, some of which featured homages to the Islamic State, often focused on Ahok's supposed unsuitability for office simply because he is a religious and ethnic minority or on other more virulent conspiracy theories that ethnically Chinese Indonesians are demographically swamping Indonesia. Many Indonesia observers believe that the groundswell of protest was a major factor that prevented Ahok, who had high popularity ratings as governor, from being elected; he lost the gubernatorial election in April 2017. The protests may also have contributed to Ahok's being jailed for two years for blasphemy, when prosecutors had not asked for such a severe sentence.[29]

The leading opposition candidate in the Jakarta election, Anies Baswedan—previously known as a relative moderate—embraced the rallies, which helped him win. Some reports suggest that leaders of the rallies were close to prominent former generals, a worrying sign in a country where civil-military relations remain precarious and Prabowo will likely run for president again in 2019. In fact, one of Prabowo's close allies appeared on the stage at many anti-Ahok rallies.

Emboldened radical groups are likely to use mass rallies to undercut Jokowi's campaign for reelection and possibly to step up recruitment for affiliates who carry out extrajudicial violence. Before Ahok's defeat, Jokowi's administration had responded to the rising militancy with confused strategies, but the president's office now considers militants a growing threat and has banned one large militant group, Hizb ut-Tahrir. The Jokowi administration has given itself new powers to ban civil society organizations that engage in radical activities.[30]

Although no terrorist network in Indonesia today appears as organized and capable as Jemaah Islamiyah was in the early 2000s, terrorists could be emboldened by rising nonviolent political aggression. Terrorist groups now also have external inspiration for their activities. The Islamic State works hard to recruit Southeast Asians; the group has released multiple social media reports in Indonesian/Malay and allowed Islamic State supporters from Southeast Asia to establish a brigade composed of Indonesian/Malay speakers in the Middle East.[31] In January 2016, militants who pledged allegiance to the Islamic State carried out a terrorist attack in Jakarta.[32] After the attack, Indonesian police arrested thirty-three people suspected to have been involved in militant groups.[33] In May 2017, three people were killed by a suicide bombing at a Jakarta bus station. The Indonesian police claim that at least one of the two suicide bombers had links to the Islamic State.[34]

Indonesian leaders also now fear that foreign fighters could be streaming into Mindanao, in the nearby southern Philippines, where Philippine troops have been engaging in a tough battle against Islamic State–affiliated militants.[35] Islamic State propaganda networks have reportedly called on fighters to travel to the southern Philippines. If fighters continue arriving in Mindanao even after the end of the battle in the city of Marawi—especially since the Islamic State has lost its territory in the Middle East—the island could easily serve as a gathering place for Indonesian extremists and a jumping-off point for militants to attack Indonesia.

The White House has become increasingly focused on radicalism in Southeast Asia. U.S. policymakers are concerned that the Islamic State sees the potential of gaining physical territory in Southeast Asia, which it could then use as a base to regroup. In addition to continuing U.S. combat in the Middle East and South Asia against Islamist radical groups, the Trump administration intends to bolster cooperation with Southeast Asian leaders to fight terrorism. U.S. officials have purposefully tried to reinvigorate relations with Southeast Asian leaders including Philippine President Duterte, Malaysian Prime Minister Najib Razak, and Thai Prime Minister Prayuth Chan-ocha, through phone calls, White House visits, and, in Duterte's case, a warm visit during Trump's November 2017 trip to Asia. While there are credible human rights concerns about the White House boosting ties with these leaders, it has done so in part to help enhance cooperation on fighting Islamic State–linked groups in Southeast Asia. In addition, the White House is boosting maritime ties with Malaysia—already a major partner in combating Islamic State–linked groups in the region—to give Malaysia greater abilities to track militants moving at sea. It also continues to provide assistance on counterterrorism strategies to the Duterte administration, despite Duterte's sometimes bombastic approach to relations with the United States.

PIRACY AND TRANSNATIONAL CRIME

Finally, the Jokowi administration has attempted to take a tougher approach to piracy and other transnational crime in Southeast Asia. Jokowi often speaks of Indonesia's need to be more effective in combating illegal activities in Southeast Asian waters, including piracy, people smuggling, drug smuggling, and illegal fishing. The Jokowi administration has made a show of capturing vessels found fishing illegally in Indonesian waters and blowing them up (after evacuating them); it has blown up more than three hundred.[36] Jokowi has made battling piracy, illegal fishing, and other illegal maritime activities a major point of discussion in his meetings with other Southeast Asian leaders.

This interest coincides with a growing U.S. interest in combating piracy and transnational crime, since piracy, human trafficking, and drug trafficking—serious threats to stability on their own—have also been sources of revenue for Islamist militant groups in Southeast Asia. The White House has issued executive orders instructing the administration to strengthen federal laws to attack transnational crime groups, including drug smugglers and people smugglers.[37] The Department of Justice has issued detailed guidance on how it plans to crack down on transnational crime organizations, including many operating in Southeast Asia.[38]

A Challenged Economic Relationship

In theory, Indonesia's sustained economic growth and demographic expansion could make it one of the biggest potential markets in the world for U.S. companies, if the two countries do not succumb to growing economic nationalism. By 2050, Indonesia will have the fourth-largest economy in the world.[39] In 2016, the American Chamber of Commerce in Jakarta released a report noting that in a best-case scenario—for example, no new bilateral trade barriers—the total value of the U.S.-Indonesia economic relationship could grow by nearly 50 percent by 2019.[40]

By 2020, more than 50 percent of the Indonesian population will have the disposable income to be considered part of a modestly affluent middle class. These Indonesians will be able to afford not only household items but also higher-end consumer products.[41] In addition, the Indonesian government has kept social media free at a time when other nations in the region, such as China, Thailand, and Vietnam, have imposed strict new regulations on internet and social media users, making them difficult places to invest for foreign internet firms and media companies. China and other states have also used a wide range of protectionist economic tactics to prevent foreign internet and social media firms from investing in the countries.

Despite this potential, though, there are significant obstacles to a more developed economic relationship between the United States and Indonesia. Jokowi himself, who has a business background, seems at times to understand that Indonesia needs to create jobs and entice investment. But the climate of economic nationalism in Indonesia is strong, and getting stronger, and similar types of economic nationalism now animate much of the Republican Party and drive White House policy.

Building on his predecessor's economic nationalism, Jokowi has tried to boost the government's influence over foreign investors. This nationalist approach is popular with many segments of the Indonesian public, but it worries many large U.S. firms and members of the U.S. Congress.[42] The Jokowi administration also initially sought the support of state-run Chinese firms in its plans to upgrade Indonesian investment, but as economic nationalism has peaked in Indonesia, Jokowi has become somewhat wary of Chinese aid and investment. Jokowi has alienated some mining and other resources companies with demands for them to refine their materials in the country and divest more of their companies to local partners. As a result, Newmont Mining exited Indonesia in 2016.[43]

The obstacles to closer economic ties exist not just on the Indonesian side. The strategic partnership the United States and Indonesia signed in 2015 established an annual ministerial-level dialogue, but the dialogue never actually commenced under the Obama administration.[44] The Trump administration has scrapped Washington's participation in the Trans-Pacific Partnership (TPP); Indonesia was not a founding member of the TPP, but Jokowi had publicly suggested Indonesia would eventually join the trade deal.[45] Under Trump, the White House has also labeled many East Asian nations, including Indonesia, potential violators of trade rules, although it has not offered concrete evidence of these claims other than noting that these nations are running trade surpluses with the United States.

Recommendations

Given that Presidents Trump and Jokowi have downplayed values-based foreign policy and that economic nationalism in both countries has hampered bilateral economic ties, it is unlikely that the United States and Indonesia will collaborate in promoting democracy in Southeast Asia or in dramatically upgrading their trade relationship in the short term, though U.S. investment in Indonesia probably will continue to rise, given the country's young and growing consumer market. The two countries' leaders should instead focus on security cooperation, where the United States and Indonesia have significant common interests. They should also take steps to ensure that the economic relationship does not deteriorate.

These shared security interests will only get stronger during the Trump administration's term. Since the Islamic State has lost most of its territory in the Middle East, some of its foreign fighters could flee, taking their views home or seeking new bases in Southeast Asia. Consequently, the threat of Islamist militancy could increase throughout Southeast Asia over the next few years. During that time, disputes over the rapid militarization of the South China Sea will likely grow, as Washington and Beijing have both signaled increasing naval assertiveness. And despite Jokowi's stated focus on piracy and other illegal maritime activities, Indonesia and other Southeast Asian nations still struggle with these nontraditional security threats.

Cooperation on these shared security interests could move the bilateral strategic relationship forward substantially. To improve strategic ties, Washington and Jakarta—assisted by Australia and other regional powers—should take the following steps.

UPGRADE BILATERAL COOPERATION ON SOUTH CHINA SEA CHALLENGES

- **The United States should increase funding for the International Military and Education Training program for Indonesian soldiers by at least 50 percent over the current amount of roughly $2.4 million annually.** This step would help solidify pro-U.S. sentiment among young officers and bolster the professionalism of the Indonesian military, which would facilitate U.S.-Indonesia security cooperation. Younger officers in the Indonesian armed forces, who have benefited from new interactions with the U.S. military since the 2000s, have gradually become willing to reconsider Jakarta's traditional adherence to nonaligned politics and a passive maritime security presence.

- **The United States should encourage Indonesia to conduct freedom of navigation operations with Australia in the South China Sea.** Indonesia and Australia likely do not want to challenge Beijing directly by conducting FONOPs alongside U.S. vessels, which would anger China more. Yet before a visit to Australia in February 2017, Jokowi publicly broached the idea of launching joint patrols in the South China Sea with Australian forces. So far, Australia has publicly resisted the idea. Indonesia and Australia should begin FONOPs together within the twelve-mile nautical zone of China's reclaimed islands in the South China Sea.

- **The United States should offer to hold joint exercises with Indonesia in waters close to the Natuna Islands.** The United States has held joint exercises in the South China Sea with other regional partners as a means of demonstrating that not only the United States but also Australia, India, Japan, and Southeast Asian nations will stand up for freedom of navigation. Holding a joint U.S.-Indonesia exercise near the Natunas would strengthen the U.S.-Indonesia security partnership and demonstrate to China that Indonesia will no longer adopt a passive approach to South China Sea concerns.

- **The United States should encourage Indonesia to meet its goal of increasing defense spending while also pushing Jokowi to upgrade Indonesia's navy and air force.** Washington should boost sales to Jakarta of larger maritime vessels, new planes, and fast coast guard ships, to help Jakarta develop maritime forces capable of protecting

Indonesian territorial waters and participating in broader actions in the South China Sea. Indonesia's force modernization should focus on the navy, coast guard, and air force, as it has no real land-based threats.

- **The United States should encourage Indonesia to take the lead in facilitating a joint ASEAN position on a code of conduct for the South China Sea.**[46] U.S. and Southeast Asian officials should encourage Jokowi and other top Indonesian leaders to highlight the 2016 Hague ruling on territorial claims in the South China Sea as a starting point for serious code negotiations. The United States should also encourage Jokowi to use ASEAN meetings in 2018 and 2019 to broker a common ASEAN position on the code of conduct.

- **The United States and Indonesia should convene their ministerial-level strategic dialogue and focus it on the South China Sea.** The Trump administration should convene the dialogue, which has not yet met. The two sides should use the dialogue to announce steps toward bilateral cooperation, such as increased U.S. support for Indonesia's military modernization and plans to hold joint U.S.-Indonesia maritime exercises near the Natunas. The strategic dialogue should also include discussions about Islamic State–linked groups in Southeast Asia, piracy and transnational crime, and the bilateral economic relationship.

BOLSTER BILATERAL STRATEGIES TO COMBAT THE ISLAMIC STATE

- **To combat the threat of Islamic State–linked attacks, the United States should help Indonesia enact more aggressive measures to locate, track, and vet returnees from Islamic State–held territory in the Middle East and identify more Indonesian militants linked to the Islamic State.** Indonesia's neighbors have had a mixed record in tracking returnees from the Islamic State. Until recently, the Jokowi administration has also been lax in tracking returnees. However, the Indonesian government could establish a formal program overseen by the police (not the military) to monitor returnees from Islamic State territory for a period of at least five years and help them be peacefully reintegrated into life in Indonesia.[47] The U.S. government could provide financial support for this reintegration program.

Regardless, the U.S. Department of the Treasury should continue to identify Indonesian militants as terrorists and impose sanctions on them by placing them on the Specially Designated Nationals and Blocked Persons List. Many more could come to Southeast Asia now that Raqqa has fallen.[48]

- **The United States should create a small, permanent force of police officers to lead foreign police trainings.** The United States is already closely involved with training the Indonesian police, but this effort is hampered by its not having a permanent unit, located within the Department of Defense, the Department of Justice, or the Department of State, for training local police forces. Such a unit—a police force that could be deployed to various countries for trainings—would bring greater experience and skill to training programs, including those aimed at combating terrorist networks.[49]

- **The United States should urge Indonesia to join the U.S.-led Global Coalition to Defeat ISIS, which would provide greater access to shared intelligence.** Given the growing menace of Islamic State–linked militants in Southeast Asia and the threat of Mindanao becoming a hub for recruits, the Jokowi administration and the White House should take stronger measures to combat the threat posed by returning Islamic State fighters. Indonesia has not yet joined the U.S.-led coalition. It also too often fails to effectively share intelligence on returnees from Iraq and Syria with other countries in the region.[50] To show that Indonesia is taking the Islamic State threat seriously, Jakarta should join the coalition.

- **Indonesia, Malaysia, and the Philippines should hold joint naval or coast guard patrols in the Sulu-Celebes Sea at least monthly; the United States should offer to join these patrols to hunt for militants.** These waters have been critical for both pirates and militants and are known historically for transnational crime and lawlessness; without sea patrols, Islamic State–linked groups will be able to move people through Southeast Asia easily. Indonesia agreed in May 2016 to begin coordinated patrols of border waters in the Sulu-Celebes Sea, along with forces from Malaysia and the Philippines.[51] However, the patrols are irregular, and their scope remains unclear.[52] The three Southeast Asian nations, along with the United States, should commit to monthly patrols, and their defense ministers should speak at least bimonthly to assess the patrols' results.

- The Jokowi administration should use the Indonesian presidency to rally public support against both violent and nonviolent militants. Tougher rhetorical measures against Islamic State–linked radicals could anger Indonesian Islamist groups like the ones that rallied against Ahok. But over 90 percent of Indonesians have an unfavorable image of the Islamic State, according to recent polling.[53] Yudhoyono used the unpopularity of violent militant groups and the popularity of Indonesia's moderate traditions and democracy to rally public support for fighting violent radicals. Jokowi, already more comfortable among religious voters than his predecessor was, could also use his platform to win public support for combating militant networks and upholding the secular, democratic nature of Indonesian institutions. Jokowi's recent declarations of support for a pluralistic Indonesia—where the government will protect citizens from violence and prevent militants from subverting democracy—provide an excellent start toward using the power of his office.

- Jokowi should reassure religious voters that he does not intend to interfere with peaceful political participation. Jokowi would thus present himself as tough on radicalism while maintaining his image as a supporter of religious rights and a friend of mainstream Muslim organizations.

COOPERATE TO COMBAT PIRACY

- The United States should offer to regularly join the Sulu-Celebes Sea patrols to provide both training and support for anti-piracy efforts. In July 2017, the U.S. Navy announced it had completed a coordinated joint patrol in the Sulu Sea with Philippine forces.[54] Regularly joining multilateral patrols would give the United States a larger stake in monitoring the Sulu Sea for militants, but a greater U.S. presence could also serve as a deterrent to pirates and other organized crime groups that have historically flourished in the Sulu waters. The United States could also join air patrols that are critical for identifying pirate boats.

- Indonesia, Malaysia, the Philippines, and the United States should use Sulu-Celebes Sea patrols to facilitate hot pursuit of pirates and militants into different nations' territorial waters. The three Southeast Asian countries, with the help of the United States, should make it easier for vessels from one nation to track pirates (or pirate/military hybrid groups) in "hot pursuit" into other nations' territorial waters. Although the countries have technically agreed to allow hot pursuit, it rarely takes place. With U.S. support, it would be easier for the Southeast Asian nations to organize and carry out hot-pursuit efforts.

TAKE LIMITED STEPS TO PROMOTE BILATERAL ECONOMIC RELATIONS

The security relationship between Jakarta and Washington has great potential and could become more robust in the next three years. The same probably cannot be said about the bilateral economic relationship, as economic nationalism is blossoming in both the United States and Indonesia. Opinion leaders in Jakarta and Washington should therefore attempt to stall any further deterioration of the bilateral economic relationship, such as through new restrictions on investment in Indonesia or U.S. tariffs on Indonesian exports.

Simply preventing the economic relationship from getting worse is a worthy goal, and could help U.S. investment into Indonesia keep growing. The White House has placed Indonesia on an initial list of countries that it believes might be abusing trade rules, confounding officials in Jakarta.[55] Yet during a visit to Indonesia in April 2017, Vice President Mike Pence softened the administration's tone toward Jakarta and raised hopes of significant progress on the bilateral trade front.[56]

The Trump administration has vowed to continue expanding U.S. markets through bilateral trade liberalization and could attempt to sign a bilateral free trade deal with Indonesia. But this is an overambitious goal when the White House is considering altering or ending trade deals with Canada, Mexico, and South Korea and when no Asian nations welcomed the idea of new bilateral deals during Trump's visit to Asia in November 2017.

Simply retaining any modest momentum in the U.S.-Indonesia economic relationship is the most viable option now. This can be accomplished in several steps.

- **The United States and Indonesia should negotiate a bilateral investment treaty in order to maintain the economic relationship.** This is a much simpler step than a bilateral trade deal, yet it would boost U.S. investment in Indonesia after the treaty is completed. Greater investment might give U.S. firms more influence over the Jokowi administration. Increased investment might also help reduce popular economic nationalism in Indonesia, if Jokowi also touted the new investment and linked it to growth, improved infrastructure, and jobs.

- **The two sides should include the U.S. Department of Commerce in the strategic dialogue and use the discussions to air concerns about the bilateral trade balance.** The dialogue itself could help ward off deterioration in the economic relationship.

- **The White House should offer a clearer public definition of abusive trading behaviors than simply running trade surpluses with the United States.** U.S. Secretary of Commerce Wilbur Ross has said the administration will investigate "the extent to which our bilateral deficit with that country [including Indonesia] is the result of cheating or other inappropriate behavior."[57] The White House should define what it considers cheating or inappropriate behavior in bilateral trade relations if it continues this investigation.

- **The United States and Indonesia should hold a high-level summit in Jakarta involving leaders of large U.S.-based multinationals, Jokowi, and other top Indonesian officials.** Such a summit could provide an opportunity for Jokowi to discuss new investments in Indonesian infrastructure, one of his biggest priorities, with U.S. companies. U.S. firms—possibly working together with Australian and Japanese companies that have familiarity with Indonesia—could be competitive bidders for the roads, rails, ports, and other infrastructure projects Indonesia desperately needs.

Conclusion

A U.S.-Indonesia strategic and economic relationship that avoids illusions and focuses on three discrete security goals—increasing deterrence in the South China Sea, combating militants linked to the Islamic State, and fighting piracy and other transnational crime in Southeast Asia—would improve regional security and advance both countries' interests.

An Indonesian government that takes a stronger stance on the South China Sea could prod ASEAN to take a more unified position overall on South China Sea disputes. In recent years, ASEAN has failed to achieve consensus on a strategy toward the South China Sea, but a stronger Indonesian position could convince other Southeast Asian nations, such as Malaysia and the Philippines, to join a unified approach.[58] Meanwhile, if Jakarta is more committed to combating the Islamic State and the piracy that increasingly fuels militant groups in Southeast Asia, Indonesia could not only become safer but also help uncover militant cells in Australia, Malaysia, the Philippines, Singapore, and other U.S. partner countries. Such a commitment might involve Indonesia upgrading its intelligence networks and sharing more information with nations in the region.

While leaders in Washington and Jakarta reshape the relationship to focus on security, the two nations should work to ensure that economic relations do not deteriorate. Any long-term U.S. economic strategy toward Southeast Asia needs to recognize that Indonesia is the largest economy in the region and the biggest untapped market for U.S. firms in Southeast Asia.

Finally, better relations with Jakarta could be an asset if Washington's relationships with other Muslim-majority nations are threatened by shifting U.S. immigration policies. Maintaining productive ties with the country that has the world's largest Muslim population could help U.S. officials argue that the new immigration policies are no barrier to working with Muslim-majority countries but simply a narrow effort to stop militants from entering the United States.

Endnotes

1. Karlis Salna and Herdaru Purnomo, "Indonesia Can't Figure Out Why It's on Trump's Trade Hit List," *Bloomberg Politics*, April 12, 2017, http://bloomberg.com/politics/articles/2017-04-12/indonesia-dazed-confused-by-u-s-trade-probe-before-pence-trip.

2. Rex Tillerson, "Remarks to U.S. Department of State Employees" (speech, U.S. Department of State, Washington, DC, May 3, 2017), http://state.gov/secretary/remarks/2017/05/270620.htm.

3. World Bank Open Data, "GDP Growth (Annual %): Indonesia," World Bank, http://data.worldbank.org/indicator/NY.GDP.MKTP.KD.ZG?locations=ID.

4. Max Walden, "Democracy in Indonesia: A Cause for Celebration," *Interpreter*, February 20, 2017, http://lowyinstitute.org/the-interpreter/democracy-indonesia-cause-celebration.

5. Adam O'Brien, "The U.S.-Indonesian Military Relationship," Council on Foreign Relations, October 3, 2005, http://cfr.org/indonesia/us-indonesian-military-relationship/p8964.

6. Fatiyah Wardah, "U.S., Indonesia Expand Military Cooperation Agreement," Voice of America, January 7, 2015, http://voanews.com/a/us-indonesia-expand-military-cooperation-agreement/2589473.html.

7. Bali Democracy Forum IX (website), Ministry of Foreign Affairs, Republic of Indonesia, http://bdf.kemlu.go.id.

8. Dewi Fortuna Anwar, "Indonesia's Foreign Relations: Policy Shaped by the Ideal of 'Dynamic Equilibrium,'" *East Asia Forum*, February 4, 2014, http://eastasiaforum.org/2014/02/04/indonesias-foreign-relations-policy-shaped-by-the-ideal-of-dynamic-equilibrium.

9. White House Office of the Press Secretary, "Joint Declaration on the Comprehensive Partnership Between the United States of America and the Republic of Indonesia," November 9, 2010, http://obamawhitehouse.archives.gov/the-press-office/2010/11/09/joint-declaration-comprehensive-partnership-between-united-states-americ.

10. White House Office of the Press Secretary, "Joint Statement by the United States of America and the Republic of Indonesia," October 26, 2015, http://obamawhitehouse.archives.gov/the-press-office/2015/10/26/joint-statement-united-states-america-and-republic-indonesia.

11. Jason Tedjasukmana, "In Indonesia, Corruption Scandals Plague Anti-Graft President," *Time*, September 26, 2011, http://content.time.com/time/world/article/0,8599,2094188,00.html.

12. Gregory Poling, "Corruption in Indonesia and the 2014 Elections," Center for Strategic and International Studies, November 7, 2013, http://csis.org/analysis/corruption-indonesia-and-2014-elections.

13. Farida Susanty, "US, Indonesia Economic Ties Set to Strengthen," *Jakarta Post*, September 16, 2016, http://thejakartapost.com/news/2016/09/16/us-indonesia-economic-ties-set-to-strengthen.html.

14. Michael Taylor and Randy Fabi, "Foreign Investors Unhappy With Some of Indonesia's New Investment Rules," Reuters, May 14, 2017, http://reuters.com/article /indonesia-economy-investment/foreign investors-unhappy-with-some-of-indonesias -new-investment-rules-idUSL3N0NV3L920140514.

15. William Pesek, "Economic Nationalism Endangers Indonesia," *Bloomberg View*, June 13, 2014, http://bloombergview.com/articles/2014-06-13/economic-nationalism -endangers-indonesia.

16. Avery Poole, "Is Jokowi Turning His Back on ASEAN?," *Diplomat*, September 7, 2017, http://thediplomat.com/2015/09/is-jokowi-turning-his-back-on-asean.

17. White House Office of the Press Secretary, "Remarks by President Trump to the 72nd Session of the United Nations General Assembly" (speech, UN General Assembly, New York, September 19, 2017), http://whitehouse.gov/the-press-office/2017/09/19 /remarks-president-trump-72nd-session-united-nations-general-assembly.

18. White House Office of the Press Secretary, "Remarks by President Trump at APEC CEO Summit" (speech, Asia-Pacific Economic Cooperation summit, Da Nang, Vietnam, November 10, 2017), https://whitehouse.gov/the-press-office/2017/11/10/remarks -president-trump-apec-ceo-summit-da-nang-vietnam.

19. "Indonesia and the South China Sea: Annoyed in Natuna," *Economist*, July 2, 2016, http://economist.com/news/asia/21701527-china-turns-would-be-peacemaker-yet -another-rival-annoyed-natuna.

20. Leila Mona Ganiem, "President Jokowi's 9 Priorities for Indonesia," *WaliZahid*, July 24, 2014, http://walizahid.com/2014/07/president-jokowis-9-priorities-for-indonesia.

21. Brian Harding and Stefanie Merchant, "Indonesia's Inward Turn," *Diplomat*, December 8, 2016, http://thediplomat.com/2016/12/indonesias-inward-turn.

22. Franz-Stefan Grady, "U.S. Clears Sale of Advanced Missiles to Indonesia," *Diplomat*, March 18, 2016, http://thediplomat.com/2016/03/us-clears-sale-of-advanced-missiles -to-indonesia.

23. Joe Cochrane, "Indonesia, Long on Sidelines, Start to Confront China's Territorial Claims," *New York Times*, September 10, 2017, http://nytimes.com/2017/09/10/world /asia/indonesia-south-china-sea-military-buildup.html.

24. Cohrane, "Indonesia, Long on Sidelines."

25. Prashanth Parameswaran, "Why Did Indonesia Just Rename Its Part of the South China Sea?," *Diplomat*, July 17, 2017, http://thediplomat.com/2017/07/why-did-indonesia -just-rename-its-part-of-the-south-china-sea/.

26. Ankit Panda, "A FONOP Schedule in the South China Sea: What Next?," *Diplomat*, September 11, 2017, http://thediplomat.com/2017/09/a-fonop-schedule-in-the-south -china-sea-what-next/.

27. Mark J. Valencia, "Trump's South China Sea Policy Taking Shape," *Japan Times*, June 23, 2017, http://japantimes.co.jp/opinion/2017/06/23/commentary/world-commentary /trumps-south-china-sea-policy-taking-shape/#.WcQlbrKGPqA.

28. "China Hits Back at Donald Trump's Remark Over South China Sea in UN Speech," AFP, September 20, 2017, http://timesofindia.indiatimes.com/world/china/china-hits -back-at-donald-trumps-barb-over-south-china-sea/articleshow/60765543.cms.

29. Kate Lamb, "Jakarta Governor Ahok Sentenced to Two Years in Prison for Blasphemy," *Guardian*, May 9, 2017, http://theguardian.com/world/2017/may/09/jakarta-governor -ahok-found-guilty-of-blasphemy-jailed-for-two-years.

30. Rieka Rahadiana, "Jokowi's New Powers to Ban Religious Groups Courts Political Risk," *Bloomberg Politics*, July 23, 2017, https://bloomberg.com/news/articles/2017-07-23 /jokowi-courts-political-risk-with-ban-on-hard-line-islamic-group.

31. Yenni Kwow, "ISIS Has Launched a Newspaper to Recruit Southeast Asian Fighters," *Time*, July 10, 2016, http://time.com/4400505/isis-newspaper-malay-southeast-asia-al -fatihin.

32. Beh Lih Yi, Oliver Holmes, and Luke Harding, "ISIS Claims Responsibility for Ja-karta Gun and Bomb Attacks," *Guardian*, January 14, 2016, http://theguardian.com/world/2016/jan/14/jakarta-bombings-multiple-casualties-after-indonesian-capital-hit-by-suicide-attacks.

33. "Indonesia Nabs ISIS-Linked Groups Planning Terror Attacks: Police Chief," AFP, February 15, 2016, http://straitstimes.com/asia/se-asia/indonesia-nabs-isis-linked-groups-planning-terror-attacks-police-chief.

34. Richard C. Paddock, "In Indonesia and the Philippines, Militants Find a Common Bond: ISIS," *New York Times*, May 26, 2017, http://nytimes.com/2017/05/26/world/asia/indonesia-philippines-isis-jakarta-marawi.html.

35. Paddock, "In Indonesia and the Philippines."

36. Prashanth Parameswaran, "Indonesia Blows Up 81 Ships in War on Illegal Fishing," *Diplomat*, April 4, 2017, http://thediplomat.com/2017/04/indonesia-blows-up-81-ships-in-war-on-illegal-fishing/.

37. Jordan Fabian, "Trump Signs Executive Actions Aimed at Crime Crackdown," *Hill*, February 9, 2017, http://thehill.com/homenews/administration/318693-trump-signs-executive-actions-targeting-crime.

38. Department of Justice Office of Public Affairs, "Department of Justice Releases Report Detailing the Prosecutions of Transnational Criminal Organizations and their Sub-sidiaries," May 5, 2017, http://www.justice.gov/opa/pr/department-justice-releases-report-detailing-prosecutions-transnational-criminal.

39. PricewaterhouseCoopers, "The World in 2050," February 2017, http://pwc.com/gx/en/issues/economy/the-world-in-2050.html.

40. Peter Milne, "Vital and Growing: Adding Up the US-Indonesia Economic Relation-ship," U.S. Chamber of Commerce, September 15, 2016, https://uschamber.com/report/report-vital-growing-adding-the-us-indonesia-economic-relationship.

41. "ASEAN in Focus: The Indonesian Consumer Market," HKTDC Research, February 15, 2017, http://hkmb.hktdc.com/en/1X0A91HG/hktdc-research/ASEAN-in-Focus-The-Indonesian-Consumer-Market.

42. Matthew Busch, "The Price of Indonesia's Economic Nationalism," *Wall Street Journal*, March 14, 2017, https://wsj.com/articles/the-price-of-indonesias-economic-nationalism-1489510058.

43. Daniel Bochove and Fitri Wulandari, "Newmont Exiting Indonesia in $1.3 Billion Sale to Local Firm," *Bloomberg*, June 30, 2016, http://bloomberg.com/news/articles/2016-06-30/newmont-and-sumitomo-enter-pact-to-sell-indonesian-mine-stake.

44. Prashanth Parameswaran, "The New U.S.-Indonesia Strategic Partnership After Jokowi's Visit: Problems and Prospects," Brookings Institution, December 8, 2015, http://brookings.edu/opinions/the-new-u-s-indonesia-strategic-partnership-after-jokowis-visit-problems-and-prospects.

45. Julie Hirschfeld Davis, "President Joko Widodo of Indonesia Joins Trans-Pacific Part-nership," *New York Times*, October 26, 2015, http://nytimes.com/2015/10/27/us/politics/president-joko-widodo-of-indonesia-joins-trans-pacific-partnership.html.

46. Manuel Mogato and Martin Petty, "Push for South China Sea Code Stirs ASEAN Sus-picions About Beijing's Endgame," Reuters, April 27, 2017, http://reuters.com/article/us-southchinasea-asean-analysis-idUSKBN17T0A5.

47. Sidney Jones, "Battling ISIS in Indonesia," *New York Times*, January 18, 2016, http://nytimes.com/2016/01/19/opinion/battling-isis-in-indonesia.html.

48. John McBeth, "Inside the Cauldron of Indonesia-ISIS Terror," *Asia Times*, January 17, 2017, http://atimes.com/article/inside-cauldron-indonesian-isis-terror.

49. Italy has such a unit and has used it effectively in many nations. See Missy Ryan, "How the Italian Police Wound Up Having a Significant Presence in Iraq," *Washington Post*,

June 23, 2016, http://washingtonpost.com/news/checkpoint/wp/2016/06/23/how-the -italian-police-wound-up-having-a-significant-presence-in-iraq/. I am grateful to Max Boot for this point.

50. Joseph Chinyong Liow, "ISIS in the Pacific: Assessing Terrorism in Southeast Asia and the Threats to the Homeland" (testimony before the House subcommittee on counterterrorism and intelligence, Washington, DC, April 27, 2016), http://brookings .edu/testimonies/isis-in-the-pacific-assessing-terrorism-in-southeast-asia-and-the -threat-to-the-homeland.

51. Joshua Kurlantzick, "Democratic Backsliding and the Reach of ISIS in Southeast Asia," *Current History* 115, no. 782 (September 2016): 226–232, http://cfr.org/content /newsletter/files/Kurlantzick.pdf.

52. "Joint Navy Patrols Between Indonesia, Philippines, and Malaysia to Cut Off Sulu Sea Corridor to Militants," Associated Press, June 4, 2017, http://scmp.com/news /asia/diplomacy/article/2096834/joint-navy-patrols-between-indonesia-philippines -and-malaysia.

53. Krithika Varagur, "Hard-Line Islamist Groups Meet Official, Popular Roadblocks in Indonesia," Voice of America, June 8, 2017, http://voanews.com/a/hard-line-islamist -groups-indonesia/3891817.html.

54. Prashanth Parameswaran, "What's With the New US-Philippines Sulu Sea Patrols Under Duterte?," *Diplomat*, July 1, 2017, http://thediplomat.com/2017/07/whats-with -the-new-us-philippines-sulu-sea-patrols-under-duterte.

55. Salna and Purnomo, "Indonesia Can't Figure Out Why It's on Trump's Trade Hit List."

56. Simon Roughneen, "Pence Softens Trump's Trade Talk During Indonesia Visit," *Nikkei Asian Review*, April 22, 2017, http://asia.nikkei.com/Politics-Economy/International -Relations/Pence-softens-Trump-s-trade-talk-during-Indonesia-visit.

57. Yashwant Raj, "Trump Orders Investigation of Countries With Trade Deficit With US, India on the List," *Hindustan Times*, April 3, 2017, http://hindustantimes.com /business-news/trump-orders-investigation-of-countries-with-trade-deficit-with-us -india-on-the-list/story-RkZjiCzHXvNmte9FbehT3L.html.

58. Manuel Mogato, Michael Martina, and Ben Blanchard, "ASEAN Deadlocked on South China Sea, Cambodia Blocks Statement," Reuters, July 26, 2016, http://reuters .com/article/us-southchinasea-ruling-asean-idUSKCN1050F6.

About the Author

Joshua Kurlantzick is senior fellow for Southeast Asia at the Council on Foreign Relations. He was previously a visiting scholar at the Carnegie Endowment for International Peace, where he studied Southeast Asian politics and economics and China's relations with Southeast Asia, including Chinese investment, aid, and diplomacy. Previously, he was a fellow at the University of Southern California's Center on Public Diplomacy and a fellow at the Pacific Council on International Policy. He is the winner of the Luce scholarship for journalism in Asia and was selected as a finalist for the Osborn Elliott Prize for journalism on Asia. He is the author of several books, including, most recently, *A Great Place to Have a War: America in Laos and the Birth of a Military CIA.*

Advisory Committee for
Keeping the U.S.-Indonesia Relationship Moving Forward

This report reflects the judgments and recommendations of the author. It does not necessarily represent the views of members of the advisory committee, whose involvement should in no way be interpreted as an endorsement of the report by either themselves or the organizations with which they are affiliated.

Mission Statement
of the Center for Preventive Action

The Center for Preventive Action (CPA) seeks to help prevent, defuse, or resolve deadly conflicts around the world and to expand the body of knowledge on conflict prevention. It does so by creating a forum in which representatives of governments, international organizations, nongovernmental organizations, corporations, and civil society can gather to develop operational and timely strategies for promoting peace in specific conflict situations. The center focuses on conflicts in countries or regions that affect U.S. interests, but may be otherwise overlooked; where prevention appears possible; and when the resources of the Council on Foreign Relations can make a difference. The center does this by

- Issuing regular reports to evaluate and respond rapidly to developing conflict situations and formulate timely, concrete policy recommendations that the U.S. government, international community, and local actors can use to limit the potential for deadly violence.

- Engaging the U.S. government and news media in conflict prevention efforts. CPA staff members meet with administration officials and members of Congress to brief on CPA's findings and recommendations; facilitate contacts between U.S. officials and important local and external actors; and raise awareness among journalists of potential flashpoints around the globe.

- Building networks with international organizations and institutions to complement and leverage the Council's established influence in the U.S. policy arena and increase the impact of CPA's recommendations.

- Providing a source of expertise on conflict prevention to include research, case studies, and lessons learned from past conflicts that policymakers and private citizens can use to prevent or mitigate future deadly conflicts.

Council Special Reports

Published by the Council on Foreign Relations

Containing Russia: How to Respond to Moscow's Intervention in U.S. Democracy and Growing Geopolitical Challenge
Robert D. Blackwill and Philip H. Gordon; CSR No. 80, January 2018

Reducing Tensions Between Russia and NATO
Kimberly Marten; CSR No. 79, March 2017
A Center for Preventive Action Report

Rebuilding Trust Between Silicon Valley and Washington
Adam Segal; CSR No. 78, January 2017

Ending South Sudan's Civil War
Kate Almquist Knopf; CSR No. 77, November 2016
A Center for Preventive Action Report

Repairing the U.S.-Israel Relationship
Robert D. Blackwill and Philip H. Gordon; CSR No. 76, November 2016

Securing a Democratic Future for Myanmar
Priscilla A. Clapp; CSR No. 75, March 2016
A Center for Preventive Action Report

Xi Jinping on the Global Stage: Chinese Foreign Policy Under a Powerful but Exposed Leader
Robert D. Blackwill and Kurt M. Campbell; CSR No. 74, February 2016
An International Institutions and Global Governance Program Report

Enhancing U.S. Support for Peace Operations in Africa
Paul D. Williams; CSR No. 73, May 2015

Revising U.S. Grand Strategy Toward China
Robert D. Blackwill and Ashley J. Tellis; CSR No. 72, March 2015
An International Institutions and Global Governance Program Report

Strategic Stability in the Second Nuclear Age
Gregory D. Koblentz; CSR No. 71, November 2014

U.S. Policy to Counter Nigeria's Boko Haram
John Campbell; CSR No. 70, November 2014
A Center for Preventive Action Report

Limiting Armed Drone Proliferation
Micah Zenko and Sarah Kreps; CSR No. 69, June 2014
A Center for Preventive Action Report

Reorienting U.S. Pakistan Strategy: From Af-Pak to Asia
Daniel S. Markey; CSR No. 68, January 2014

Afghanistan After the Drawdown
Seth G. Jones and Keith Crane; CSR No. 67, November 2013
A Center for Preventive Action Report

The Future of U.S. Special Operations Forces
Linda Robinson; CSR No. 66, April 2013

Reforming U.S. Drone Strike Policies
Micah Zenko; CSR No. 65, January 2013
A Center for Preventive Action Report

Countering Criminal Violence in Central America
Michael Shifter; CSR No. 64, April 2012
A Center for Preventive Action Report

Saudi Arabia in the New Middle East
F. Gregory Gause III; CSR No. 63, December 2011
A Center for Preventive Action Report

Partners in Preventive Action: The United States and International Institutions
Paul B. Stares and Micah Zenko; CSR No. 62, September 2011
A Center for Preventive Action Report

Justice Beyond The Hague: Supporting the Prosecution of International Crimes in National Courts
David A. Kaye; CSR No. 61, June 2011

The Drug War in Mexico: Confronting a Shared Threat
David A. Shirk; CSR No. 60, March 2011
A Center for Preventive Action Report

UN Security Council Enlargement and U.S. Interests
Kara C. McDonald and Stewart M. Patrick; CSR No. 59, December 2010
An International Institutions and Global Governance Program Report

Congress and National Security
Kay King; CSR No. 58, November 2010

Toward Deeper Reductions in U.S. and Russian Nuclear Weapons
Micah Zenko; CSR No. 57, November 2010
A Center for Preventive Action Report

Internet Governance in an Age of Cyber Insecurity
Robert K. Knake; CSR No. 56, September 2010
An International Institutions and Global Governance Program Report

From Rome to Kampala: The U.S. Approach to the 2010 International Criminal Court Review Conference
Vijay Padmanabhan; CSR No. 55, April 2010

Strengthening the Nuclear Nonproliferation Regime
Paul Lettow; CSR No. 54, April 2010
An International Institutions and Global Governance Program Report

The Russian Economic Crisis
Jeffrey Mankoff; CSR No. 53, April 2010

Somalia: A New Approach
Bronwyn E. Bruton; CSR No. 52, March 2010
A Center for Preventive Action Report

The Future of NATO
James M. Goldgeier; CSR No. 51, February 2010
An International Institutions and Global Governance Program Report

The United States in the New Asia
Evan A. Feigenbaum and Robert A. Manning; CSR No. 50, November 2009
An International Institutions and Global Governance Program Report

Intervention to Stop Genocide and Mass Atrocities: International Norms and U.S. Policy
Matthew C. Waxman; CSR No. 49, October 2009
An International Institutions and Global Governance Program Report

Enhancing U.S. Preventive Action
Paul B. Stares and Micah Zenko; CSR No. 48, October 2009
A Center for Preventive Action Report

The Canadian Oil Sands: Energy Security vs. Climate Change
Michael A. Levi; CSR No. 47, May 2009
A Maurice R. Greenberg Center for Geoeconomic Studies Report

The National Interest and the Law of the Sea
Scott G. Borgerson; CSR No. 46, May 2009

Lessons of the Financial Crisis
Benn Steil; CSR No. 45, March 2009
A Maurice R. Greenberg Center for Geoeconomic Studies Report

Global Imbalances and the Financial Crisis
Steven Dunaway; CSR No. 44, March 2009
A Maurice R. Greenberg Center for Geoeconomic Studies Report

Eurasian Energy Security
Jeffrey Mankoff; CSR No. 43, February 2009

Preparing for Sudden Change in North Korea
Paul B. Stares and Joel S. Wit; CSR No. 42, January 2009
A Center for Preventive Action Report

Averting Crisis in Ukraine
Steven Pifer; CSR No. 41, January 2009
A Center for Preventive Action Report

Congo: Securing Peace, Sustaining Progress
Anthony W. Gambino; CSR No. 40, October 2008
A Center for Preventive Action Report

Deterring State Sponsorship of Nuclear Terrorism
Michael A. Levi; CSR No. 39, September 2008

China, Space Weapons, and U.S. Security
Bruce W. MacDonald; CSR No. 38, September 2008

Sovereign Wealth and Sovereign Power: The Strategic Consequences of American Indebtedness
Brad W. Setser; CSR No. 37, September 2008
A Maurice R. Greenberg Center for Geoeconomic Studies Report

Securing Pakistan's Tribal Belt
Daniel S. Markey; CSR No. 36, July 2008 (web-only release) and August 2008
A Center for Preventive Action Report

Avoiding Transfers to Torture
Ashley S. Deeks; CSR No. 35, June 2008

Global FDI Policy: Correcting a Protectionist Drift
David M. Marchick and Matthew J. Slaughter; CSR No. 34, June 2008
A Maurice R. Greenberg Center for Geoeconomic Studies Report

Dealing with Damascus: Seeking a Greater Return on U.S.-Syria Relations
Mona Yacoubian and Scott Lasensky; CSR No. 33, June 2008
A Center for Preventive Action Report

Climate Change and National Security: An Agenda for Action
Joshua W. Busby; CSR No. 32, November 2007
A Maurice R. Greenberg Center for Geoeconomic Studies Report

Planning for Post-Mugabe Zimbabwe
Michelle D. Gavin; CSR No. 31, October 2007
A Center for Preventive Action Report

The Case for Wage Insurance
Robert J. LaLonde; CSR No. 30, September 2007
A Maurice R. Greenberg Center for Geoeconomic Studies Report

Reform of the International Monetary Fund
Peter B. Kenen; CSR No. 29, May 2007
A Maurice R. Greenberg Center for Geoeconomic Studies Report

Nuclear Energy: Balancing Benefits and Risks
Charles D. Ferguson; CSR No. 28, April 2007

Nigeria: Elections and Continuing Challenges
Robert I. Rotberg; CSR No. 27, April 2007
A Center for Preventive Action Report

The Economic Logic of Illegal Immigration
Gordon H. Hanson; CSR No. 26, April 2007
A Maurice R. Greenberg Center for Geoeconomic Studies Report

The United States and the WTO Dispute Settlement System
Robert Z. Lawrence; CSR No. 25, March 2007
A Maurice R. Greenberg Center for Geoeconomic Studies Report

Bolivia on the Brink
Eduardo A. Gamarra; CSR No. 24, February 2007
A Center for Preventive Action Report

After the Surge: The Case for U.S. Military Disengagement From Iraq
Steven N. Simon; CSR No. 23, February 2007

Darfur and Beyond: What Is Needed to Prevent Mass Atrocities
Lee Feinstein; CSR No. 22, January 2007

Avoiding Conflict in the Horn of Africa: U.S. Policy Toward Ethiopia and Eritrea
Terrence Lyons; CSR No. 21, December 2006
A Center for Preventive Action Report

Living with Hugo: U.S. Policy Toward Hugo Chávez's Venezuela
Richard Lapper; CSR No. 20, November 2006
A Center for Preventive Action Report

Reforming U.S. Patent Policy: Getting the Incentives Right
Keith E. Maskus; CSR No. 19, November 2006
A Maurice R. Greenberg Center for Geoeconomic Studies Report

Foreign Investment and National Security: Getting the Balance Right
Alan P. Larson and David M. Marchick; CSR No. 18, July 2006
A Maurice R. Greenberg Center for Geoeconomic Studies Report

Challenges for a Postelection Mexico: Issues for U.S. Policy
Pamela K. Starr; CSR No. 17, June 2006 (web-only release) and November 2006

U.S.-India Nuclear Cooperation: A Strategy for Moving Forward
Michael A. Levi and Charles D. Ferguson; CSR No. 16, June 2006

Generating Momentum for a New Era in U.S.-Turkey Relations
Steven A. Cook and Elizabeth Sherwood-Randall; CSR No. 15, June 2006

Peace in Papua: Widening a Window of Opportunity
Blair A. King; CSR No. 14, March 2006
A Center for Preventive Action Report

Neglected Defense: Mobilizing the Private Sector to Support Homeland Security
Stephen E. Flynn and Daniel B. Prieto; CSR No. 13, March 2006

Afghanistan's Uncertain Transition From Turmoil to Normalcy
Barnett R. Rubin; CSR No. 12, March 2006
A Center for Preventive Action Report

Preventing Catastrophic Nuclear Terrorism
Charles D. Ferguson; CSR No. 11, March 2006

Getting Serious About the Twin Deficits
Menzie D. Chinn; CSR No. 10, September 2005
A Maurice R. Greenberg Center for Geoeconomic Studies Report

Both Sides of the Aisle: A Call for Bipartisan Foreign Policy
Nancy E. Roman; CSR No. 9, September 2005

Forgotten Intervention? What the United States Needs to Do in the Western Balkans
Amelia Branczik and William L. Nash; CSR No. 8, June 2005
A Center for Preventive Action Report

A New Beginning: Strategies for a More Fruitful Dialogue with the Muslim World
Craig Charney and Nicole Yakatan; CSR No. 7, May 2005

Power-Sharing in Iraq
David L. Phillips; CSR No. 6, April 2005
A Center for Preventive Action Report

*Giving Meaning to "Never Again": Seeking an Effective Response to the Crisis
in Darfur and Beyond*
Cheryl O. Igiri and Princeton N. Lyman; CSR No. 5, September 2004

Freedom, Prosperity, and Security: The G8 Partnership with Africa: Sea Island 2004 and Beyond
J. Brian Atwood, Robert S. Browne, and Princeton N. Lyman; CSR No. 4, May 2004

Addressing the HIV/AIDS Pandemic: A U.S. Global AIDS Strategy for the Long Term
Daniel M. Fox and Princeton N. Lyman; CSR No. 3, May 2004
Cosponsored with the Milbank Memorial Fund

Challenges for a Post-Election Philippines
Catharin E. Dalpino; CSR No. 2, May 2004
A Center for Preventive Action Report

Stability, Security, and Sovereignty in the Republic of Georgia
David L. Phillips; CSR No. 1, January 2004
A Center for Preventive Action Report

Note: Council Special Reports are available for download from CFR's website, www.cfr.org.
For more information, email publications@cfr.org.